NATIONAL GEOGRAPHIC

Potatoes

Beatrice Duggan

Did you know that farmers plant potatoes in the ground?
New potatoes grow from these old potatoes.

3

Farmers use machines to plant potatoes.
They plant the potatoes in rows.

5

New potato plants grow from
the old potatoes that were planted.
The plants are green and leafy.

7

Flowers grow on the potato plants.
Potatoes grow under the ground.

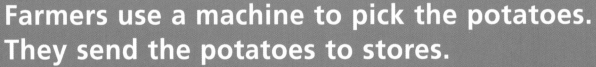

Farmers use a machine to pick the potatoes. They send the potatoes to stores.

11

We buy the potatoes to eat. Yum!